Exceptional
Latinos

EVA LONGORIA

*Actress
and
Businesswoman*

Maria Betances

Enslow Publishing
101 W. 23rd Street
Suite 240
New York, NY 10011
USA

enslow.com

Words to Know

audition—A short performance to show the talents of someone who is being considered for a role.

charity—A group that helps people in need.

Chicano—An American with Mexican parents or grandparents.

documentary—A movie or TV program that presents facts about real people, events, or issues.

immigration—Entering into a new country to settle there.

inspiration—Something that encourages someone to do something.

nominate—To suggest somebody for an honor or position.

philanthropist—A person who gives money and time to help make life better for other people.

production company—A company that makes movies.

Contents

Eva Longoria

CHAPTER 1

Texas Childhood

Eva Longoria is many things to many people. She is an actress, spokesperson, writer, **philanthropist**, and businesswoman. She is also a proud Latina.

Eva Jacqueline Longoria was born on March 15, 1975, in Corpus Christi, Texas. Her family had strong roots in Mexico as well as Texas. Eva was the youngest of four girls. Her father worked on an army base, and her mother was a teacher for children with special needs. Though her parents spoke Spanish,

Eva sometimes calls herself a "Texican" or Mexican American because of her family's deep roots in both Mexico and Texas.

Eva Says:

"We're ninth-generation Americans. We never crossed the border; the border crossed us. We've owned the same ranch land since 1603."

they did not teach their children how to do so because schools told them not to.

Even though her family often had little money, Eva had a normal childhood. In high school, she worked at a fast food restaurant and taught exercise classes. She went to Texas A&M University at Kingsville where she studied kinesiology, or human movement.

Eva thought her first trip to Los Angeles would be a fun vacation. She never thought that she would become a famous actress.

Eva had planned to go on to study exercise science and sports medicine, but something happened in 1998 that changed her life. Eva entered the Miss Corpus Christi beauty contest. She won a trip to Los Angeles, California, to enter a talent contest there. She won and decided to be an actress.

CHAPTER 2

Desperate Housewife

Eva began taking acting classes and going on **auditions**. She was not an instant star. She had small parts on television shows including *Beverly Hills, 90210; Ally McBeal*; and *General Hospital.* Life was not easy. She worked long hours for little pay.

Finally, Eva won a role on a soap opera called *The Young and the Restless*. She played her part for two years before her character was sent to

Eva Says:

"One time I called home crying. I had no money. My mom sent me $20 in the mail. But I was born with optimism."

an insane asylum. Eva said, "I had a great time on [the show], and it obviously led me to better things."

One of Eva's "better things" came in 2004. She got a role on *Desperate Housewives*, a TV show that became a major hit. Her character, Gabrielle Solis, was a fan favorite. Suddenly,

Eva poses with her costars of the hit TV show *Desperate Housewives*.

Thanks to her role on *Desperate Housewives*, Eva became famous.

Eva was a star. She was named one of the most beautiful people on the planet by *People* magazine and was **nominated** for a Golden Globe award for her acting.

CHAPTER 3

Eva's Causes

Desperate Housewives ran until 2012. After the show, Eva went back to school. She received a degree in **Chicano** studies and political science. Eva is very interested in issues that affect Latinos such as **immigration** laws and conditions for farm workers. This is why she often works with groups like the United Farm Workers and the Mexican American Legal Defense Educational Fund. She learned how to speak Spanish so she could connect better with other Latinos too.

Eva also works with PADRES Contra El Cáncer, a **charity** that helps children with cancer. Once,

Eva spoke at the Democratic National Convention in 2012. She is very involved in political causes that affect Latinos in the United States.

Eva's sister Liza (right) has always been an important part of her life.

she gave her pay for an episode of *Desperate Housewives* to the group—about $440,000.

Eva has started her own groups to aid special causes too. The Eva Longoria Foundation supports the education of Latina women as well as helping them begin their own businesses. Eva also cofounded Eva's Heroes to help people with disabilities. This is a cause close to her

Eva attends a charity event with some friends.
Helping other people is very important to her.

heart. Her older sister Liza was born with special needs. Liza has always been a source of **inspiration** to Eva.

For all of these efforts and more, Eva was named Philanthropist of the Year by *The Hollywood Reporter* newspaper in 2009. She has not slowed down her charitable works since then.

Eva Says:

"I was blessed with a sister who has special needs. Now, I work to impact the lives of similar young adults nationwide."

CHAPTER 4

Successful Businesswoman

Even though she is busy with other interests, Eva has never given up acting. She has appeared in the TV show *Brooklyn Nine-Nine* and voiced a character on the cartoon *Mother Up!* She also chooses movie roles that capture her interest, such as 2014's *Frontera*.

Eva also works behind the scenes of popular shows. She owns a **production company** called UnbeliEVAble Entertainment, which created hits like *Devious Maids*. She has also produced two

Eva starred in the movie *Frontera*. The story takes place on the border between Arizona and Mexico.

documentaries on farm workers and another on voting in the Latino community.

Eva has another interest: cooking. She is a talented cook and often makes meals for friends and loved ones. In 2008 she opened a restaurant

Eva has found happiness and success doing the many things that she loves.

in Hollywood called Beso. Beso (which means "kiss" in Spanish) serves Tex-Mex food, including two of Eva's special recipes: guacamole and tortilla soup. She even wrote a bestselling cookbook called *Eva's Kitchen: Cooking with Love for Family and Friends.*

Eva Longoria has had success in Hollywood and beyond. Some even wonder if Eva will run for political office in the future! No matter what she decides, her many passions and excellent business sense will continue to guide her future choices.

Eva Says:

"I always knew that I'm gonna have to work hard. Nothing's gonna be given to me."

Timeline

1975—Eva Jacqueline Longoria is born March 15 in Corpus Christi, Texas.

1998—Eva wins the Miss Corpus Christi beauty contest.

2000—Eva appears on her first TV show, *Beverly Hills, 90210*.

2001—Eva lands a role on *The Young and the Restless*.

2004—Eva gets a starring role on *Desperate Housewives*.

2006—Eva founds the charity Eva's Heroes.

2008—Eva opens her restaurant Beso.

2009—Eva is named Philanthropist of the Year by *The Hollywood Reporter*.

2010—Eva starts the Eva Longoria Foundation.

2011—Eva releases her cookbook *Eva's Kitchen: Cooking with Love for Family and Friends*.

2012—Eva speaks at the Democratic National Convention.

2014—Eva releases the documentary *Food Chains* about farm workers.

Learn More

Books

Adam, Alma Flor, and Isabel Campoy. *Yes! We Are Latinos!* Watertown, Mass.: Charlesbridge, 2013.

Depietro, Frank. *Mexican Americans*. Broomall, Pa.: Mason Crest, 2012.

Longoria, Eva, and Marah Stets. *Eva's Kitchen: Cooking with Love for Family & Friends*. New York: Clarkson Potter, 2011.

Schulte, Mary. *Eva Longoria*. Broomall, Pa.: Mason Crest, 2009.

Web Sites

evasheroes.org

Find out how Eva's Heroes helps young people with special needs.

evalongoriafoundation.org

Learn more about the Eva Longoria Foundation and its support of Latinas in business and education.

Index

Published in 2016 by Enslow Publishing, LLC.
101 W. 23rd Street, Suite 240, New York, NY 10011

Copyright © 2016 by Enslow Publishing, LLC.

All rights reserved.

No part of this book may be reproduced by any means without the written permission of the publisher.

Cataloging-in-Publication Data

Betances, Maria.
Eva Longoria: actress and businesswoman / by Maria Betances.
p. cm. — (Exceptional Latinos)
Includes bibliographical references and index.
ISBN 978-0-7660-6708-0 (library binding)
ISBN 978-0-7660-6706-6 (pbk.)
ISBN 978-0-7660-6707-3 (6-pack)
1. Longoria, Eva, —1975-. 2. Actors and actresses—United States—Biography—Juvenile literature. 3. Actors—United States—Biography—Juvenile literature. I. Title.
PN2287.L6325 B483 2016
791.43028—d23

Printed in the United States of America

To Our Readers: We have done our best to make sure all Web site addresses in this book were active and appropriate when we went to press. However, the author and the publisher have no control over and assume no liability for the material available on those Web sites or on any Web sites they may link to. Any comments or suggestions can be sent by e-mail to customerservice@enslow.com.

Photo Credits: Alexander Tamargo/Getty images Entertainment/Getty Images, p. 20; Jeff Kravitz/FilmMagic/Getty Images, p. 11; Darren Abate/Invision for Xbox 360/AP Images, p. 15; Frederick M. Brown/Getty Images, pp. 4, 16; © Magnolia Pictures/courtesy Everett Collection, p. 19; Robert Mora/Getty Images Entertainment/Getty Images, p. 6; Robyn Beck/AFP/Getty Images, p.14; SGranitz/WireImage/Getty images, p. 8; Sipa via AP Images, p. 12; Toria/Shutterstock.com (blue background).

Cover Credits: a berti/Marka/SuperStock.com (Eva Longoria); Toria/Shutterstock.com (blue background).